**Erica Fortgens**

# Creative Embroidery on Paper

Cantecleer

# TABLE OF CONTENTS

Distributor for books, tools and kits:
Ecstasy Crafts
PO Box 525
Watertown, NY
13601 USA

Ecstasy Crafts
630 Shannonville Rd
Shannonville, ON
KOK 3AO Canada

Toll free order line **888-288-7131**
Fax 613-968-7876
e-mail info@ecstasycrafts.com
www.ecstasycrafts.com

© 2001 Cantecleer, Baarn

Cover: Erik Uitenbogaard
Photography: Studio Wim Burgsteijn, Ede
Printing: Van der Weij BV Grafische Bedrijven, Hilversum
Translation: Cindi Beckman, Studio Imago

ISBN 90 213 3177 2

# INTRODUCTION

This third volume of *Embroidery on Paper* contains ideas
for making creative, fun cards for every occasion. There
are Christmas trees and angels and cards for Easter. This
book includes cards for children and gift labels, as well as
festive cards for Valentine's Day. Some cards are easy to
make, though a number of designs are for those with a
really steady hand, as the holes are located very close
together, making precise hole piercing (using a ruler, for
instance) essential. Should the holes run into each other
nonetheless, you can always stick a piece of adhesive tape
to the back and simply start piercing all over again.

## Materials
- Piercing tool fine Erica with embroidery needle
- Piercing tool Erica with embroidery needle
- Piercing tool coarse Erica with embroidery needle
- Piercing mat
- Erica's square cards (embossing paper)
- Erica's rectangle cards (embossing paper)
- Thread: Coats sewing machine embroidery thread
- Adhesive tape
- Scissors
- Glue
- Aslan or double-sided tape
- Ruler

If you should wish to combine the embrodery with em-
bossing, the follwing embossing templates are available:
Square: Decorative, Elegant, Geometrical and Romantic.
Rectangle: Passe-partout, Flower and Heart, Victorian,
Ornamental.

## Technique and tips
Photocopy the pattern, place it on the piercing mat and
pierce the holes. Place the pattern where desired on the
card and adhere it using a few pieces of adhesive tape.
Next, place it on the piercing mat. Pierce the pattern into
the card. Hold the card against the light to see whether
you have pierced all holes.

## Embroidery
Follow the instructions step by step. For example, insert
behind A and pull the thread through the card, leaving a
piece of thread behind. Secure the end of the thread with
adhesive tape (without blocking the pierced holes).

Please note: The threads that run across the back of the card are indicated in the descriptions by numbers in parentheses. For example, 1-2 = across the front and (2-3) = across the back.

## The stem stitch is done as follows

1-2 (2-3)   3-4 (4-5)   5-6 etc.

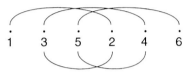

You always skip two holes on top and one hole underneath. To obtain a nice curve, embroider along the inside of the curve. If the curve is not working out right, add a stitch.

## Fastening the sequins

Insert behind the card at the point where the sequin should be fastened. Pull the thread through and then through a bead. Pull the thread back through the sequin and card. When making eyes and noses, make a knot at the end of the thread. Next, pull the thread through the front of the card and secure it to the back using adhesive tape. Snip off the extra thread on the other side of the knot.

## The needle

The needle must always be pulled through the hole vertically and pulled through the card from the front or behind. Do not start pulling the needle through the next hole before you've pulled it through the first one, as this will result in creases in the paper. Pull the thread not too tightly and not too loosely. Keep a towel on hand to wipe off your hands to prevent grease spots from getting on the cards.

You will sometimes have to rethread through the same hole; make a loop at the back, pull the thread through the loop and then rethread through the same hole. Some patterns have corners on which the holes are close together. It is not possible to number everything to scale. The diagram on page 5 shows the pattern for corners and curves.

## The corner principle

Always connect the numbered holes of the one line with the same numbered holes of the other. In other words: A1-B1!

Corner I is a closed corner. This means that point 0 is connected to AI and BI0.

Corner 2 is an open corner. This means that hole 0 does not get pierced and is not connected to AI or BI0.

*Corner I example*

| Across front | Across back |
|---|---|
| AI - BI | BI - B2 |
| B2 - A2 | A2 - A3 |
| A3 - B3 | B3 - B4 |
| B4 - A4 | A4 - A5 |
| A5 - B5 | B5 - B6 |
| B6 - A6 | A6 - A7 |
| A7 - B7 | B7 - B8 |
| B8 - A8 | A8 - A9 |
| A9 - B9 | B9 - BI0 |
| BI0 - AI0 | AI0 - 0 |
| 0 - AI | AI - 0 |
| 0 - BI0 | |

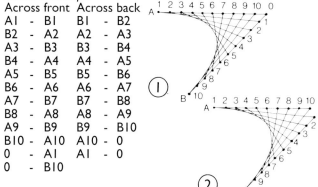

## The curve principle

If there is an uneven number of holes, we call this a closed curve. There will therefore be 9 holes and the outermost threads will meet at 5.

*Technique*

| Across front | Across back |
|---|---|
| 1-5 | 5-6 |
| 6-2 | 2-3 |
| 3-7 | 7-8 |
| 8-4 | 4-5 |
| 5-9 | |

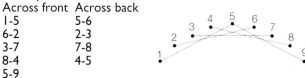

If there is an even number of holes, we call this an open curve.

*Technique*

| Across front | Across back |
|---|---|
| 1-5 | 5-6 |
| 6-2 | 2-3 |
| 3-7 | 7-8 |
| 8-4 | |

## Finishing

To cover up the back of the card, glue a card of the same size and colour to it. Good luck!

**Erica Fortgens**

# I. CHRISTMAS DESIGNS

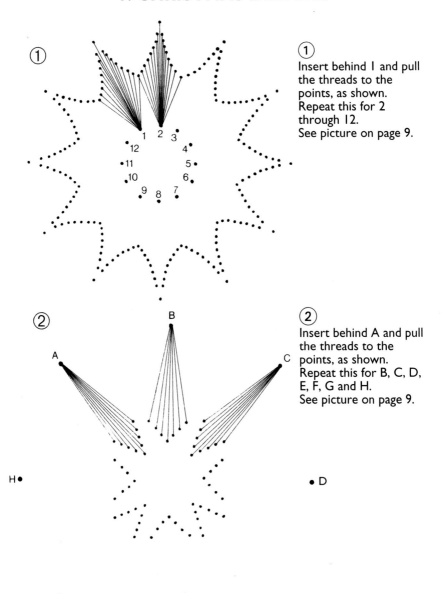

① 
Insert behind I and pull the threads to the points, as shown.
Repeat this for 2 through 12.
See picture on page 9.

② 
Insert behind A and pull the threads to the points, as shown.
Repeat this for B, C, D, E, F, G and H.
See picture on page 9.

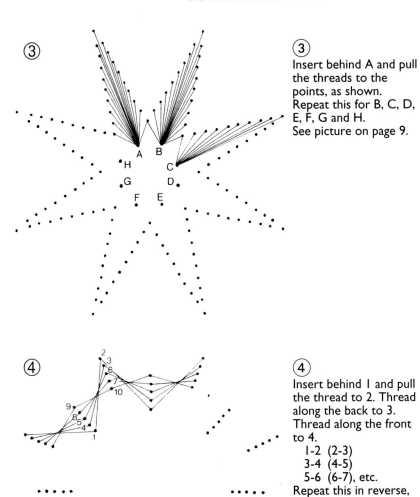

③ Insert behind A and pull
the threads to the
points, as shown.
Repeat this for B, C, D,
E, F, G and H.
See picture on page 9.

④ Insert behind 1 and pull
the thread to 2. Thread
along the back to 3.
Thread along the front
to 4.
   1-2  (2-3)
   3-4  (4-5)
   5-6  (6-7), etc.
Repeat this in reverse,
thus completing the
circle.
See picture on page 9.

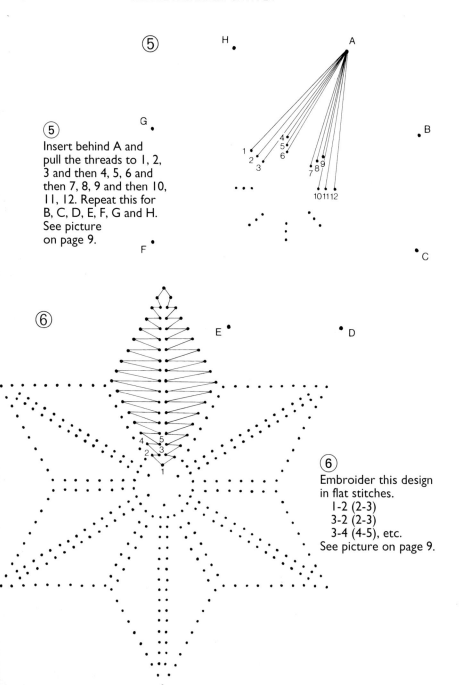

⑤

H

A

⑤ Insert behind A and pull the threads to 1, 2, 3 and then 4, 5, 6 and then 7, 8, 9 and then 10, 11, 12. Repeat this for B, C, D, E, F, G and H. See picture on page 9.

G

B

1 2 3 4 5 6 7 8 9 10 11 12

F

C

⑥

E

D

⑥ Embroider this design in flat stitches.
1-2 (2-3)
3-2 (2-3)
3-4 (4-5), etc.
See picture on page 9.

4 5 2 3 1

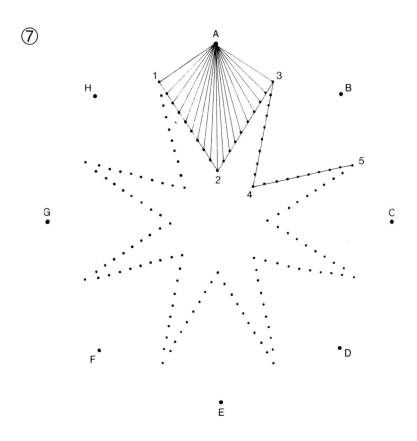

⑦
Insert behind A and pull the threads to all
points lying opposite, as shown. Repeat this for
B, C, D, E, F, G and H. Now connect points 1,
2, 3, 4, 5, etc. by pulling threads between them.
See picture on page 9.

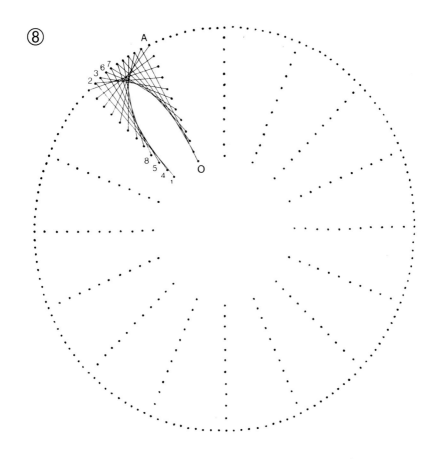

⑧

⑧
Insert behind I and pull the thread to 2. Thread
along the back to 3 and then along the front to 4.
   I-2 (2-3)
   3-4 (4-5)
   5-6 (6-7), etc.
Until you arrive at 0.
Start the next curve from 0. Once you have
completed all curves, pull a thread from A to 0
across the holes. See picture on page 9.

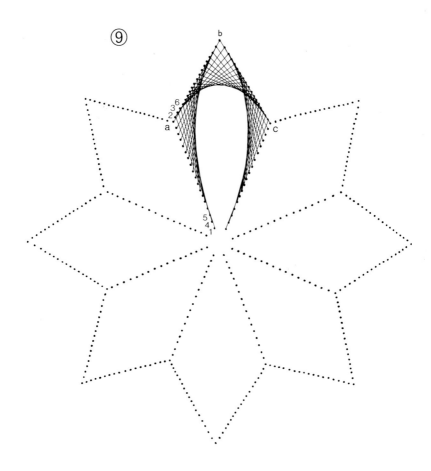

⑨

Insert behind 1 and pull the thread to 2. Thread
along the back to 3 and then along the front to 4.
   1-2 (2-3)
   3-4 (4-5)
   5-6, etc.
Note: points a, b and c are skipped. Finish all
corners and then connect points a, b and c to
one another with threads. See picture on page 9.

## 2. CHRISTMAS TREES

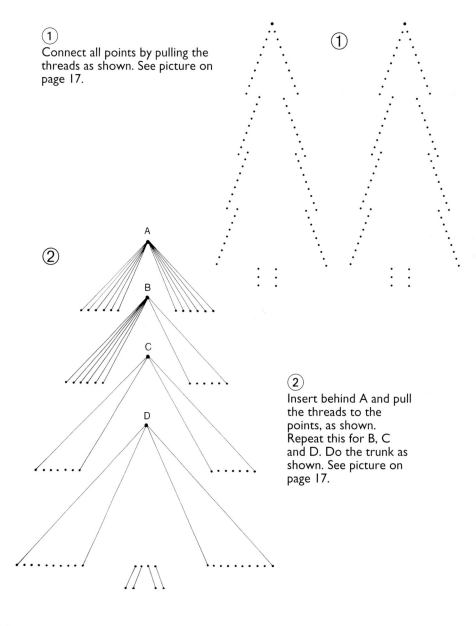

① Connect all points by pulling the threads as shown. See picture on page 17.

①

②

② Insert behind A and pull the threads to the points, as shown. Repeat this for B, C and D. Do the trunk as shown. See picture on page 17.

③

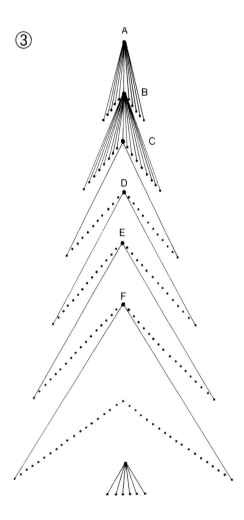

A

B

C

D

E

F

③
Insert behind A and pull
the threads to the points,
as shown. Repeat this for
B, C, D, E and F. Do the
trunk as shown. See
picture on page 17.

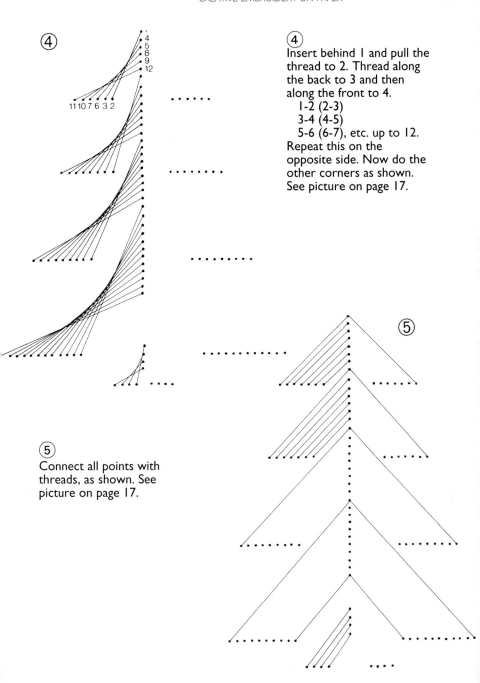

④

Insert behind 1 and pull the thread to 2. Thread along the back to 3 and then along the front to 4.
1-2 (2-3)
3-4 (4-5)
5-6 (6-7), etc. up to 12. Repeat this on the opposite side. Now do the other corners as shown. See picture on page 17.

⑤

Connect all points with threads, as shown. See picture on page 17.

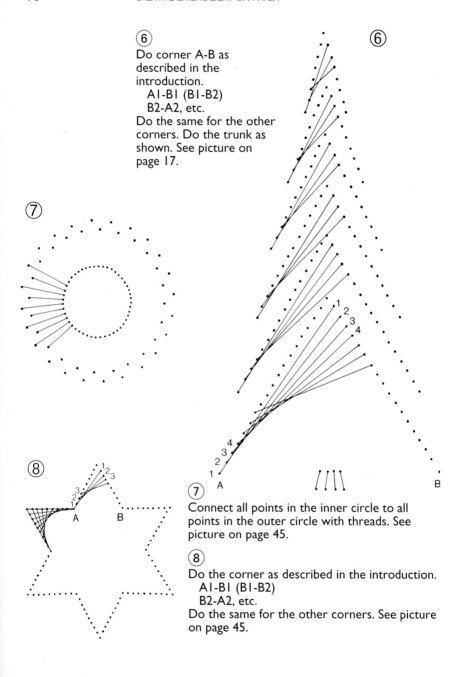

(6)
Do corner A-B as
described in the
introduction.
  A1-B1 (B1-B2)
  B2-A2, etc.
Do the same for the other
corners. Do the trunk as
shown. See picture on
page 17.

(7)
Connect all points in the inner circle to all
points in the outer circle with threads. See
picture on page 45.

(8)
Do the corner as described in the introduction.
  A1-B1 (B1-B2)
  B2-A2, etc.
Do the same for the other corners. See picture
on page 45.

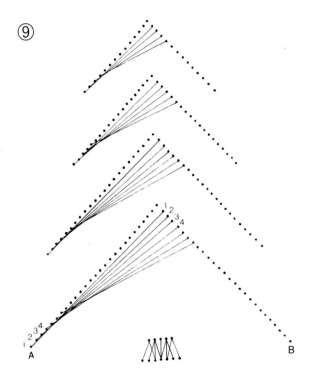

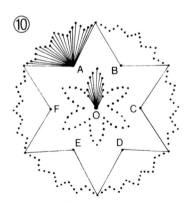

### ⑨

Do corner A-B as described in the introduction.
  A1-B1 (B1-B2)
  B2-A2, etc.
Do the same for the other corners. Do the trunk as shown. See picture on page 17.

### ⑩

Insert behind 0 and pull the threads to all points surrounding it. Insert behind A and pull the threads to all points, as shown. Repeat this for B, C, D, E and F. See picture on page 45.

## 3. CHRISTMAS ANGELS

### ①

Pull threads from A and B for the wings, as shown. Pull threads from 1, 2, 3 and 4 as shown. Do the face in stem stitch. Cut approx. 30 threads measuring 4 cm each. Lay them down at point X and sew them down. Attach sequins to the points shown. See picture on page 21.

### ②

Insert behind A and pull the threads to all points surrounding it. Connect the points with thread.
See picture on page 45.

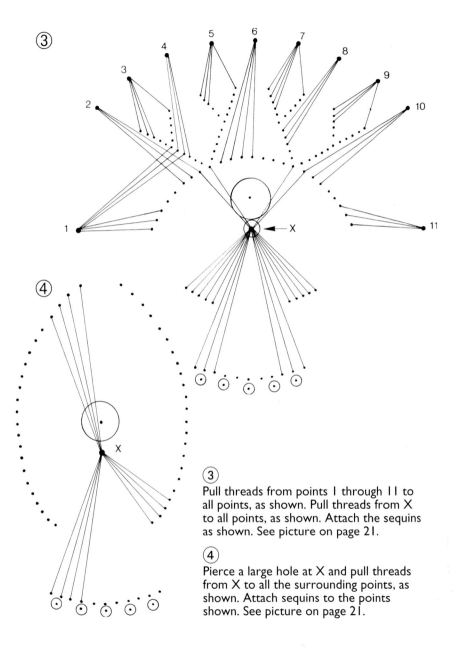

③
Pull threads from points 1 through 11 to all points, as shown. Pull threads from X to all points, as shown. Attach the sequins as shown. See picture on page 21.

④
Pierce a large hole at X and pull threads from X to all the surrounding points, as shown. Attach sequins to the points shown. See picture on page 21.

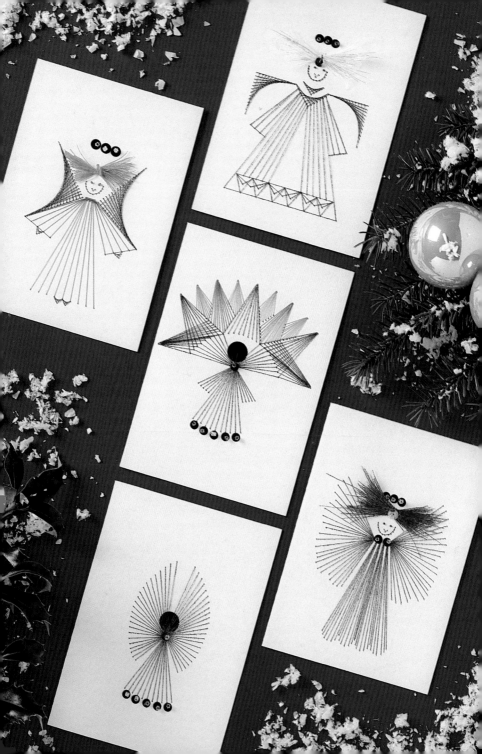

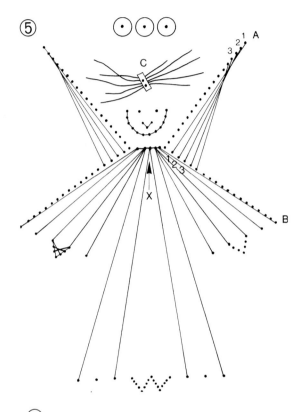

⑤

Embroider the wings.
 A1-B1 (B1-B2)
 B2-A2, etc.
Do the hands and feet using the same
technique. Make an elongated hole at point X,
from which you pull threads to the points
shown. Cut approx. 20 threads measuring 3 cm
each and lay them down at point C. Sew them
down. Attach the sequins and beads at the
points shown. Do the face in stem stitch. Cut
20 threads measuring around 4 cm each and
attach them at the point shown.
See picture on page 21.

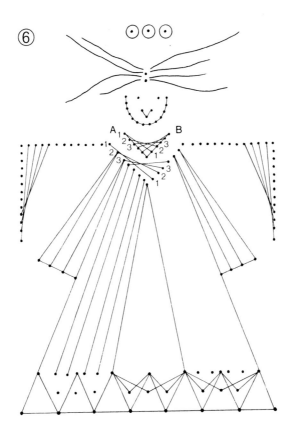

(6)

Embroider the corners of the wings and the two corners in the middle as described in the introduction.

A1-B1 (B1-B2)
B2-A2 (A2-A3), etc.

Do the face in stem stitch and the dress by pulling the threads, as shown. Do the border in zigzag stitch as shown. Embroider the face in stem stich. Cut 20 threads measuring around 5 cm and attach them at the point shown. See picture on page 21.

# 4. FESTIVE CARDS WITH SHINY THREAD

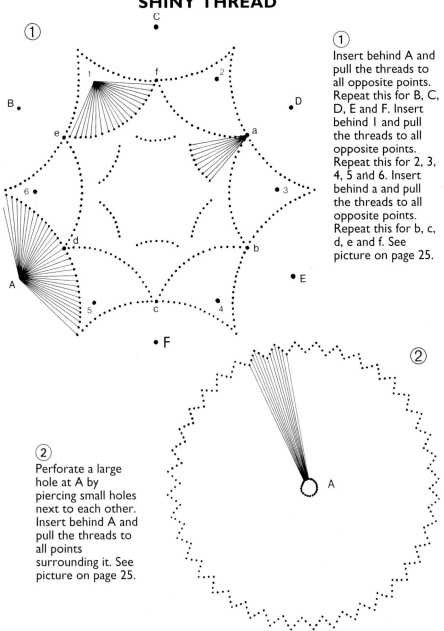

① Insert behind A and pull the threads to all opposite points. Repeat this for B, C, D, E and F. Insert behind I and pull the threads to all opposite points. Repeat this for 2, 3, 4, 5 and 6. Insert behind a and pull the threads to all opposite points. Repeat this for b, c, d, e and f. See picture on page 25.

② Perforate a large hole at A by piercing small holes next to each other. Insert behind A and pull the threads to all points surrounding it. See picture on page 25.

③
Connect the points
in the inner circle
with the points in
the outer circle, as
shown. See picture
on page 25.

④
Insert behind A and pull the
threads to 1, 2 and 3. From
B, pull to 2, 3 and 4. From C
to 3, 4 and 5. From D to 4, 5
and 6, etc. until you have
completed the circle. See
picture on page 25.

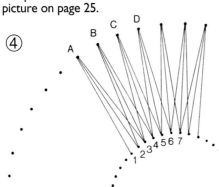

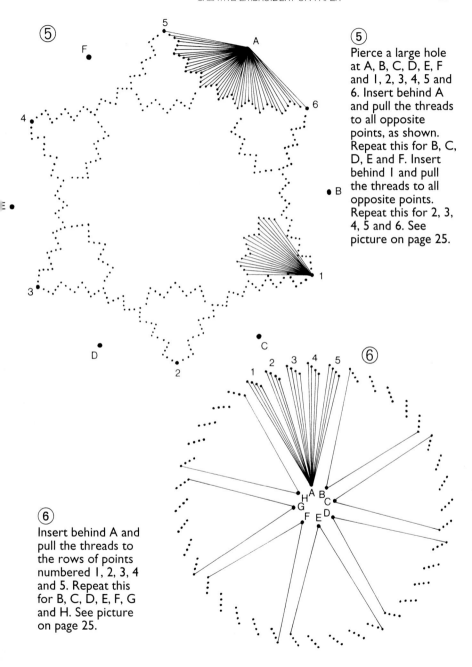

⑤

Pierce a large hole at A, B, C, D, E, F and 1, 2, 3, 4, 5 and 6. Insert behind A and pull the threads to all opposite points, as shown. Repeat this for B, C, D, E and F. Insert behind 1 and pull the threads to all opposite points. Repeat this for 2, 3, 4, 5 and 6. See picture on page 25.

⑥

Insert behind A and pull the threads to the rows of points numbered 1, 2, 3, 4 and 5. Repeat this for B, C, D, E, F, G and H. See picture on page 25.

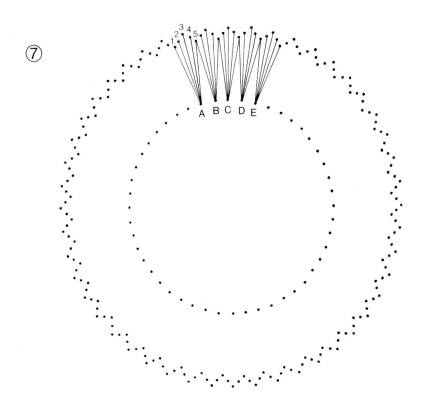

⑦

Insert behind A and pull the threads to the five opposite points. Repeat this for B, C, D, E, etc. until the circle is complete. See picture on page 25.

# 5. STRING ART ON PAPER IN BLUE

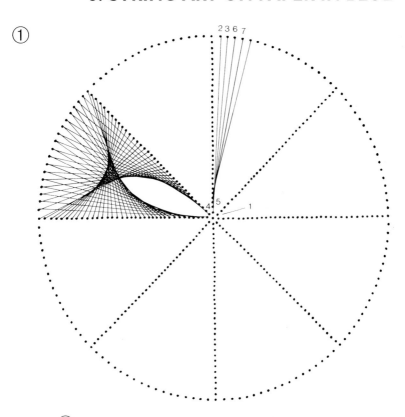

① 
This is a pattern for those with a really steady hand because the holes are located extremely close together. Should the holes run into each other when piercing, stick a piece of adhesive tape to the back and start piercing once again. Point I is the centre. Insert behind I and pull the thread to 2. Thread along the back to 3 and then along the front to 4.

 I-2 (2-3)
 3-4 (4-5)
 5-6 (6-7), etc. until you arrive back at I.

Do the same for the seven other curves. See picture on page 33.

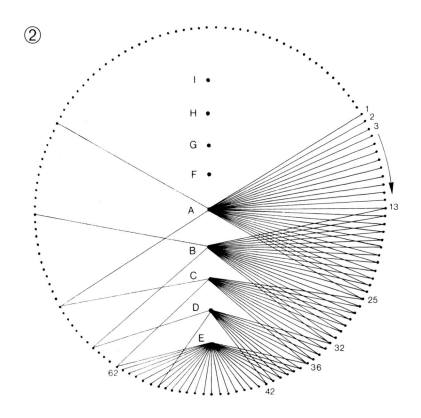

②

Insert behind A and pull the threads to 1 through 25.
Repeat this on the other side. Insert behind B and pull
the threads to 13 through 32. Repeat this on the other
side and from point F. Insert behind C and pull the
threads to 25 through 35. Repeat this on the other
side and from point G. Insert behind D and pull the
threads to 32 through 42. Repeat this on the other
side and from point H. insert behind E and pull the
threads to 36 through 62. Repeat this from point I.
See picture on page 33.

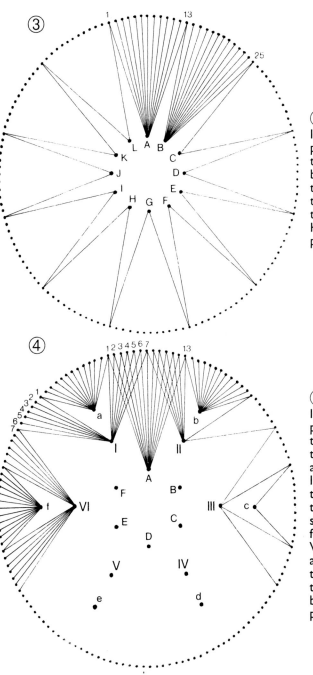

③
Insert behind A and pull the threads to 1 through 13. Insert behind B and pull the threads to 13 through 25. Repeat this for C, D, E, F, G, H, I, J, K and L. See picture on page 33.

④
Insert behind A and pull the threads to 1 through 13. Repeat this for B, C, D, E and F. Insert behind I and pull the threads to 1 through 7 on both sides. Repeat this for II, III, IV, V and VI. Insert behind a and pull the threads to all points from 1 to 1. Repeat this for b, c, d, e and f. See picture on page 33.

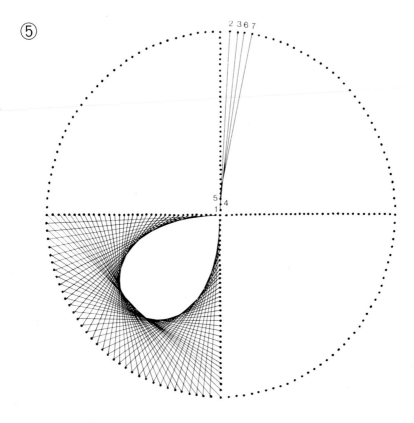

⑤
This is a pattern for accurate piercers! Point 1 is
the centre. Insert behind 1 and pull the thread
to 2. Thread along the back to 3 and then along
the front to 4.
    1-2 (2-3)
    3-4 (4-5)
    5-6, etc. until you arrive back at 1.
Do the same for the three other curves. See
picture on page 33.

# 6. EASTER AND SPRING CARDS

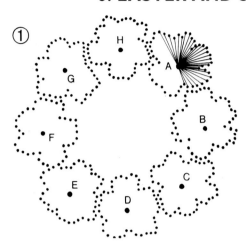

①

**①**

Insert behind A and pull the threads to all the surrounding points. Repeat this for B, C, D, F, G and H. See picture on page 37.

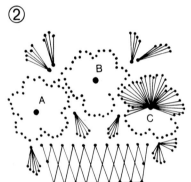

②

**②**

Insert behind A and pull the threads to all the surrounding points. Repeat this for B and C. Do the leaves as shown. Do the basket in a flat stitch, as shown. See picture on page 37.

③

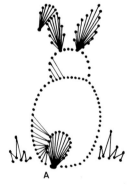

**③**

Do the blades of grass as shown. Embroider the tail by pulling the threads from A to the surrounding points. Do the body by connecting the points of the tail with the surrounding points. Do the same for the head. Do the ears as shown. Use a double stranded thread. See picture on page 37.

④
Do the blades of grass, beaks and legs as shown. Insert behind A and pull the threads to all points surrounding it. Embroider the head. Do the same for all the chicks. See picture on page 37.

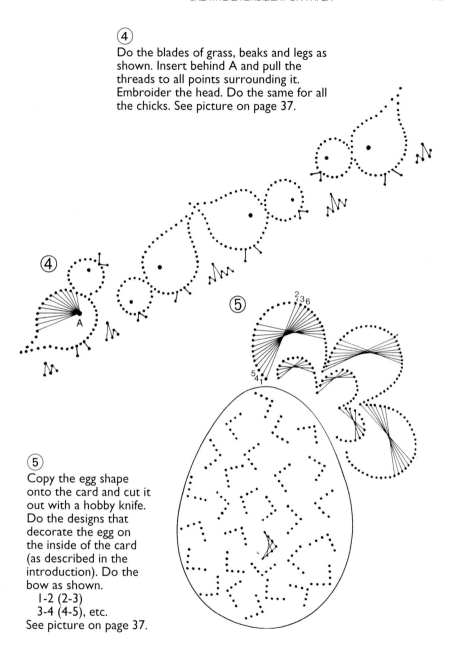

④

A

⑤

⑤
Copy the egg shape onto the card and cut it out with a hobby knife. Do the designs that decorate the egg on the inside of the card (as described in the introduction). Do the bow as shown.
   1-2 (2-3)
   3-4 (4-5), etc.
See picture on page 37.

# 7. STRING ART ON PAPER IN YELLOW

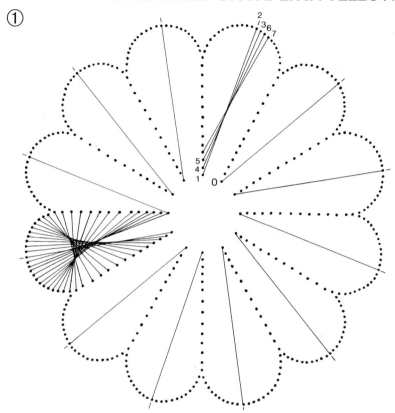

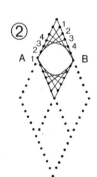

### ①

Insert behind 1 and pull the thread to 2. Thread along the back to 3 and then along the front to 4.
    1-2 (2-3)
    3-4 (4-5) until you arrive at point 0.
Do the same for all the curves. See picture on page 41.

### ②

Do the corner as described in the introduction.
    A1-B1 (B1-B2)
    B2-A2 (A2-A3), etc.
Do the same for the other corners. See picture on page 45.

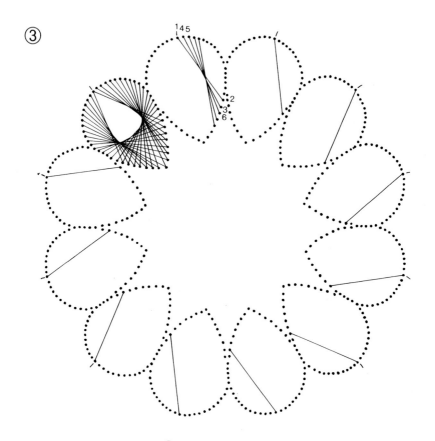

③

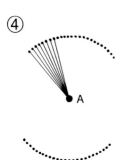

④

③
Insert behind 1 and pull the thread to 2.
Thread along the back to 3 and then along
the front to 4.
   1-2 (2-3)
   3-4 (4-5), etc. until you arrive back at 1.
Do the same for the other curves. See
picture on page 41.

④
Insert behind A and pull the threads to
all the surrounding points. See picture on
page 45.

⑤

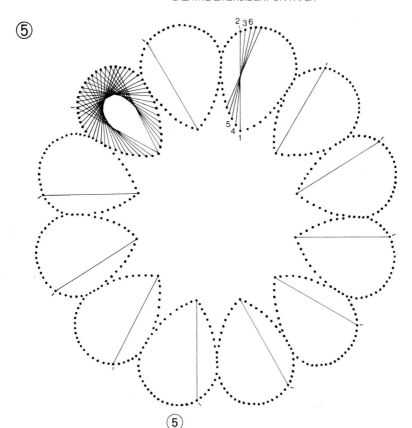

⑤
Insert behind 1 and pull the thread to 2.
Thread along the back to 3 and then along
the front to 4.
   1-2 (2-3)
   3-4 (4-5), etc. until you arrive back at 1.
Do the same for all other curves. See
picture on page 41.

⑥

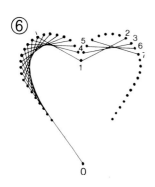

⑥
Insert behind 1 and pull the thread to 2.
Thread along the back to 3 and then along
the front to 4.
   1-2 (2-3)
   3-4 (4-5), etc. until you arrive at point 0.
Do the same on the other side. See picture
on page 45.

⑦

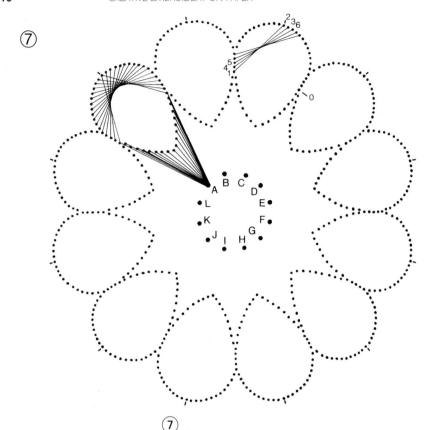

⑦
Insert behind 1 and pull the thread to 2. Thread along the back to 3 and then along the front to 4.
  1-2 (2-3)
  3-4 (4-5), etc. until you arrive at 0.
Do the same for the other curves. Insert behind A and pull the threads to the points lying opposite, as shown. Repeat this for B, C, D, E, F, G, H, I, J, K and L. See picture on page 41.

⑧

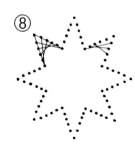

⑧
Do the corner as described in the introduction.
  A1-B1 (B1-B2)
  B2-A2 (A2-A3), etc.
Do the same for the other corners. See picture on page 45.

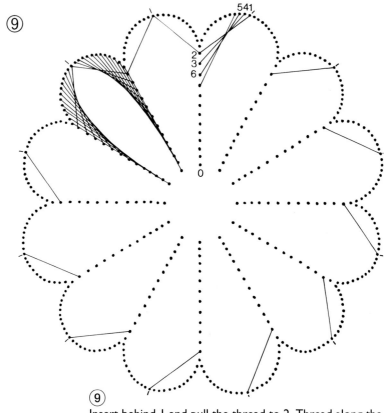

⑨

Insert behind 1 and pull the thread to 2. Thread along the back to 3 and then along the front to 4.

1-2 (2-3)
3-4 (4-5), etc. until you arrive at point 0.

Next, insert again behind 1 and do the other half of the curve. Do the same for all the other curves. See picture on page 41.

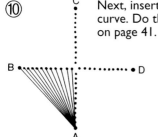

⑩

Insert behind A and pull the threads to the points, as shown. Repeat this for B, C and D. See picture on page 45.

# 8. CARDS FOR CHILDREN

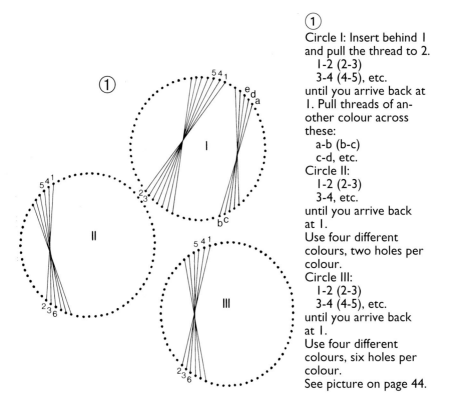

(1)
Circle I: Insert behind I
and pull the thread to 2.
   1-2 (2-3)
   3-4 (4-5), etc.
until you arrive back at
I. Pull threads of an-
other colour across
these:
   a-b (b-c)
   c-d, etc.
Circle II:
   1-2 (2-3)
   3-4, etc.
until you arrive back
at I.
Use four different
colours, two holes per
colour.
Circle III:
   1-2 (2-3)
   3-4 (4-5), etc.
until you arrive back
at I.
Use four different
colours, six holes per
colour.
See picture on page 44.

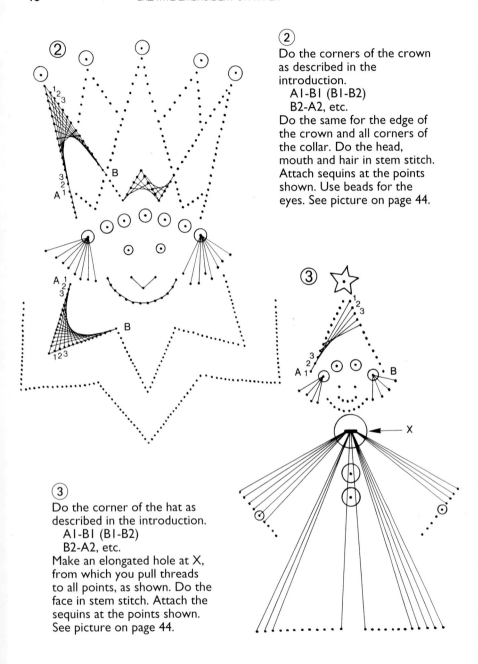

②
Do the corners of the crown
as described in the
introduction.
  A1-B1 (B1-B2)
  B2-A2, etc.
Do the same for the edge of
the crown and all corners of
the collar. Do the head,
mouth and hair in stem stitch.
Attach sequins at the points
shown. Use beads for the
eyes. See picture on page 44.

③
Do the corner of the hat as
described in the introduction.
  A1-B1 (B1-B2)
  B2-A2, etc.
Make an elongated hole at X,
from which you pull threads
to all points, as shown. Do the
face in stem stitch. Attach the
sequins at the points shown.
See picture on page 44.

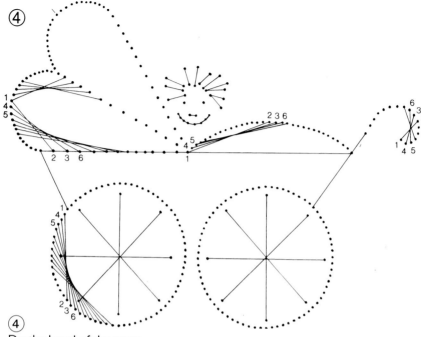

④
Do the hood of the pram.
   1-2 (2-3)
   3-4 (4-5), etc.
Do the same for the blanket and handle of the pram, as shown. Use a different coloured thread every two holes for the blanket. Do the spokes by connecting the points as shown.
Do the wheels:
   1-2 (2-3)
   3-4 (4-5), etc.
Do the child's head in stem stitch, as shown. See picture on page 44.

⑤　• B

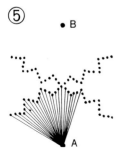

⑤
Insert behind A and pull the threads to all points, as shown. Repeat this for B. See picture on page 45.

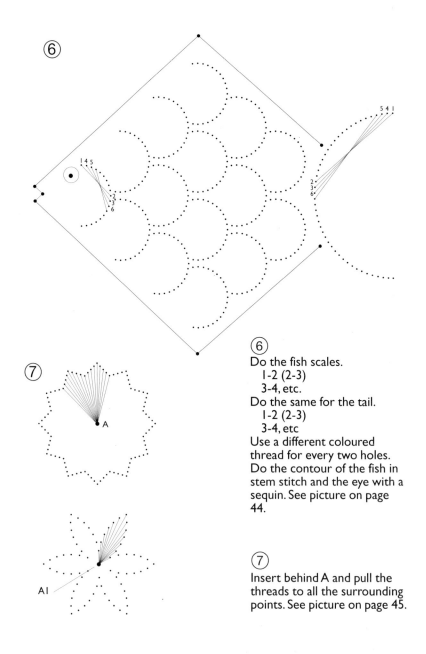

⑥
Do the fish scales.
  1-2 (2-3)
  3-4, etc.
Do the same for the tail.
  1-2 (2-3)
  3-4, etc
Use a different coloured
thread for every two holes.
Do the contour of the fish in
stem stitch and the eye with a
sequin. See picture on page
44.

⑦

Insert behind A and pull the
threads to all the surrounding
points. See picture on page 45.